MONEY

ACKNOWLEDGMENTS

To Jack Stockman
of Oak Park, Illinois,
for the art work
on the cover.

To Erika Tiepel
of Littleton, Colorado,
for the layout
and design.

To Zondervan Bible Publishers
for permission to use
the NIV text,
The Holy Bible: New International Version
©1973, 1978, 1984 by International Bible Society.
Used by permission of Zondervan Bible Publishers.

MONEY
HANDLING THE BUCKS

PETER MENCONI, RICHARD PEACE,
& LYMAN COLEMAN

DEVELOPED BY
SERENDIPITY
H O U S E

DISTRIBUTED BY
NAVPRESS ®
A MINISTRY OF THE NAVIGATORS

QUESTIONS ABOUT THIS COURSE FOR AN

ENTRY LEVEL SUPPORT GROUP

PURPOSE

1. **What is this course all about?** Becoming a support group while studying the Bible.

SEEKERS/ STRUGGLERS

2. **Who is it for?** Two kinds of people: (a) Seekers who do not know where they are with God but are open to finding out, and (b) Strugglers who are committed to Jesus Christ but need to grow in their faith.

ABY BOOMERS

3. **Who is this course specifically designed for?** While the course is for everyone, the series is primarily written for Baby Boomers.

NEW PEOPLE

4. **Does this mean that I can invite my "non-church" friends?** Absolutely, this is what this group is all about—giving people a chance to restart their spiritual pilgrimage.

STUDY

5. **What are we going to study?** Six views of finance (see inside front cover) and what the Bible has to say about each one.

AUTHORS

6. **Who wrote the material?** Peter Menconi (dentist/consultant/free-lance writer), Richard Peace (seminary professor and free-lance consultant on media), and Lyman Coleman (group process trainer and writer).

DREAM

7. **What motivated us to write this course?** A dream to offer to Baby Boomers and others the chance to investigate the Christian life for a few weeks in a support group.

FIRST SESSION

8. **What do we do at the meetings?** In the first session, you get acquainted and decide on one of two Bible study tracks. In sessions two through seven, you follow the track you chose.

TWO TRACKS

9. **What are the two tracks?** Gospel Study or Epistle Study. The Gospel Study is a more basic, "entry-level" study with a questionnaire with multiple choice options. (None of the options are "right" or "wrong." They are designed to start you thinking.) The Epistle Study has open-ended questions which usually necessitate more involvement in the Scripture text.

5

CHOOSING

10. Which track of Bible study do you recommend? The Gospel Study is best for newly-formed groups or groups that are unfamiliar with small group Bible study. The Epistle Study is best for deeper Bible study groups.

BOTH

11. Can you choose both? Yes, depending upon your time schedule.

Here's how to decide:

STUDY	APPROXIMATE COMPLETION TIME
Gospel Study only	40–60 minutes
Epistle Study only	40–60 minutes
Gospel and Epistle Study	80–120 minutes

HOMEWORK OPTION

12. What if we want to do both the Gospel and Epistle Studies but don't have time at the session? You can spend two weeks on a unit—the Gospel Study the first week and the Epistle Study the next. Or, you can do the Gospel Study in the session and the Epistle Study for homework.

BIBLE KNOWLEDGE

13. What if you don't know anything about the Bible? No problem. The Gospel Study is based on a parable or story that stands on its own—to discuss as though you are hearing it for the first time. The Epistle Study comes with complete Reference Notes—to keep you up to speed.

THE FEARLESS FOURSOME
HOW TO OVERCOME GROUP JITTERS!

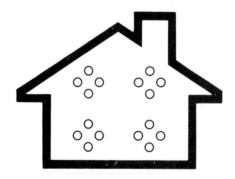

PROBLEM: A lot of people are afraid of groups.

SOLUTION: Divide into groups of 4 when the time comes for sharing. In 4's the quiet person will be able to talk, and the talkative person will not dominate as much. In fact, in 4's most of the problems of group dynamics will be avoided.

SO: When the time comes for sharing, ask 4 to sit around the dining table, 4 around the kitchen table, and 4 around a folding table in the family room.

14. What is the purpose of the Reference Notes in the Epistle Study?
To help you understand the context of the Bible passage and any difficult words that need to be defined.

15. Who leads the meetings? One person can lead for the whole time—or you can rotate the leadership.

16. What are the ground rules for the group?

☐ Priority: While you are in the course, you give the group meetings priority.

☐ Participation: Everyone participates and no one dominates.

☐ Respect: Everyone is given the right to their own opinion and "dumb questions" are encouraged and respected.

☐ Confidentiality: Anything that is said in the meeting is never repeated outside the meeting.

☐ Empty Chair: The group stays open to new people at every meeting as long as they understand the ground rules.

☐ Support: Permission is given to call upon each other in time of need —even in the middle of the night.

17. What happens to the group after finishing the course? The group is free to disband or continue to another course.

SESSION 1
Introduction

Money commands a central place in many of our lives. We dream about having more; we worry about not having enough. Money to most of us is more than paper and change. It is the basis of our well-being. We give meaning to money which goes far beyond its ability to purchase goods and services.

For some of us, money means security (especially for those who experienced the Great Depression). We may squirrel away money for those ominous rainy days or stash cash for a "safe" retirement. Others of us see money as a way of obtaining self-worth. After all, isn't money life's report card? We usually esteem people who have large amounts of money. We make them our leaders—in government, in business, and in the church. Still others sadly equate money with affection. Money and gifts may be given as a substitute for love or given with "strings attached."

Jesus understood the allure of money and spoke about it often. In the following studies, we will see that while money is not overtly evil, it is often abused. As an alternative, Jesus teaches that money is a tool to be used to further God's kingdom. In addition, the Epistle passages give us further guidance in the proper use of money.

FYI

For Your Information
- The richest 1% of Americans own about 35% of the national wealth.
- 93% of surveyed teenage girls deemed shopping to be their favorite pastime—way ahead of sixth-rated dating.
- There are slightly more poor people living in America's rural areas than live in our big cities.
- Children constitute the poorest age group in the United States. (In 1986, one out of every five children lived below the poverty line. The percentages increase for children under the age of six.)

LEADER: IF YOU HAVE MORE THAN SEVEN AT THE MEETING, SUBDIVIDE INTO GROUPS OF FOUR FOR GREATER PARTICIPATION (SEE BOX ON PAGE 6).

Orientation: In the first session, take some time to review the questions and answers on pages 5–7 about this course, especially the RULES for a support group.

OPEN

1. If you had a lot of money, how would you use it? I would . . .

   ___ buy a new house   ___ use it for my own ministry
   ___ buy a new car(s)   ___ take a long vacation
   ___ make high-risk investments   ___ give it to my kids
   ___ make low-risk investments   ___ do nothing different
   ___ retire   ___ spend it
   ___ start or buy a business   ___ save it
   ___ give it to charity/church   ___ other _____

2. Which one of the following best describes your attitude toward poor people?

   ___ they are to be pitied
   ___ they are just like you and me
   ___ they are lazy
   ___ they have gotten "a raw deal"
   ___ they aren't very smart
   ___ they need a break
   ___ they should be supported by our government
   ___ they should be put to work
   ___ they are free-loaders
   ___ they are exploited
   ___ they will always be with us

3. Have you ever lost a large amount of money? How did it make you feel?

   ___ empty   ___ upset
   ___ discouraged   ___ crushed
   ___ unnerved   ___ angry
   ___ no different   ___ humiliated
   ___ miserable   ___ sick
   ___ worthless   ___ stupid
   ___ panicked   ___ foolish
   ___ embarrassed   ___ depressed

4. Which one of the following statements best describes you as an "investor"?

   ___ I like to take high risks
   ___ I like to take calculated risks
   ___ I'm a conservative investor
   ___ I invest time, not money
   ___ I got "burned" too many times
   ___ I play it safe
   ___ I like "get-rich-quick" investments

5. Have you ever made an investment (of either money, time, or energy) which you now regret? Why do you regret it and what would you now do differently?

6. If you could do anything, how would you invest the rest of your life?

REFLECT

STEP TWO: As time allows, discuss with your group your agreement or disagreement with the following statements.

● The more money, the less virtue.

— Henry David Thoreau

● Money becomes a way of defining who you are by what you have.

— Maury Klein

● Our pocketbooks have more to do with heaven and also with hell than our hymnbooks.

— Helmut Thielicke

SESSION 2
High Finance

In 1830 Alexis de Tocqueville wrote that "the love of wealth is . . . at the bottom of all that the Americans do." Over 150 years later, this statement still holds true. Although we do not like to admit it, "The American Dream" is primarily the pursuit of a better life through improving our economic position. We are inundated with books and newspaper and magazine articles which tell us how to make and keep more money. We fantasize about doubling our income. We dream of winning the lottery or a sweepstakes contest so we can be "set for life."

Despite the fact that Americans have one of the highest standards of living in the world, we want more. But does more bring us happiness or bring us closer to God? When Mother Teresa was visiting the United States, she was asked to comment on her impressions of America. She stated that while India was mired in tremendous physical poverty, America experienced widespread spiritual poverty.

Money has always been important to people. Jesus understood the attraction of money and how it can produce greed. In the Gospel passage, Jesus tells us how to be freed from the grip of greed. He teaches that more money does not make one better in God's sight and often makes one worse. In the Epistle Study, James warns us about oppressing other people with our money. The warning: God plays "hardball" too.

OPTION 1

Gospel Study/The Almighty Buck

OPEN

STEP ONE: Answer the following questions and share your responses with your group.

**LEADER:
IF YOU HAVE
⎰RE THAN SEVEN
⎰T THE MEETING,
SUBDIVIDE
⎰NTO GROUPS OF
FOUR FOR
GREATER
PARTICIPATION
(SEE BOX ON
PAGE 6).**

1. When you were in your dating years, what were you known for?
   ____ "doing up the town"   ____ "going Dutch"
   ____ going on "cheap dates"   ____ conveniently forgetting your wallet

2. In buying Christmas presents, what is your financial guideline?
   ____ necessities only, no luxuries
   ____ only what people couldn't have afforded themselves
   ____ nothing over $10
   ____ nothing but the best
   ____ enough to compensate other people for what they'll spend on me

3. Are you a home-owner or renter? Why?

4. How many TVs are in your household? How many were in the home where you grew up?

STEP TWO: Read Luke 12:13-21 and discuss your responses to the following questions with your group.

> *¹³Someone in the crowd said to him, "Teacher, tell my brother to divide the inheritance with me."*
>
> *¹⁴Jesus replied, "Man, who appointed me a judge or an arbiter between you?" ¹⁵Then he said to them, "Watch out! Be on your guard against all kinds of greed; a man's life does not consist of the abundance of his possessions."*
>
> *¹⁶And he told them this parable: "The ground of a certain rich man produced a good crop. ¹⁷He thought to himself, 'What shall I do? I have no place to store my crops.'*
>
> *¹⁸"Then he said, 'This is what I'll do. I will tear down my barns and build bigger ones, and there I will store all my grain and my goods. ¹⁹And I'll say to myself, "You have plenty of good things laid up for many years. Take life easy; eat, drink, and be merry."*
>
> *²⁰"But God said to him, 'You fool! This very night your life will be demanded from you. Then who will get what you have prepared for yourself?'*
>
> *²¹"This is how it will be with anyone who stores up things for himself but is not rich toward God."*   Luke 12:13-21 NIV

1. In terms of "barn-building," how would you compare yourself? Why?
   a. Mine are bigger or more numerous than my parents
   b. Mine are smaller or less numerous than my parents
   c. My children, in turn, will have it "bigger and better" than me
   d. My children, in turn, will have it "not as good" as me
   e. I've scaled up my standard of living from where I was 5 years ago
   f. I've scaled down my living standard from where I was 5 years ago

2. Why did the man want to get Jesus involved in money matters?
   a. He considered Jesus to be a financial expert
   b. He was trying to make Jesus look foolish
   c. He was frustrated and was searching for answers
   d. He thought Jesus could solve the problem

3. What did Jesus mean by "all kinds of greed"?
   a. Amassing as much money as possible
   b. Winning at all costs
   c. Being "money-hungry"
   d. Picking the pockets of other people

4. What is meant by the saying, "a man's life does not consist in the abundance of his possessions"?
   a. Don't try to make money because it's meaningless
   b. The best things in life are free
   c. Materialism keeps you from true living
   d. Chasing after "things" is a dead-end street
   e. The one with the most toys doesn't win
   f. There is more to life than money

5. What do you think is Jesus' attitude toward "getting ahead"?
   a. It's okay as long as no one else gets hurt
   b. It's wrong if it is for selfish reasons
   c. "Get ahead" for God and not yourself
   d. Greater wealth brings greater responsibility

6. In what ways are Americans today similar to the rich man?
   a. We like to enjoy the "fruits of our labor"
   b. We want to amass as many possessions as possible
   c. We are oriented to "the good life"
   d. We consider ourselves before we consider God

7. Why was God's reaction to the rich man so severe?
   a. Because God is intolerant of self-indulgence
   b. Because God is jealous of other "gods" such as money
   c. Because God wants us to "seek first his kingdom"
   d. Because God doesn't like rich people

8. Which one of the following statements best describes your reaction to this parable?
   a. I am personally offended by it
   b. I really don't understand it
   c. I totally agree with it
   d. I learned something from it
   e. I disagree with God's response

APPLY   **STEP THREE: Answer the following questions and discuss your responses with your group.**

1. If Jesus took a look at your checking account, what do you think he would say?

2. If you had more money, how would you use it?

3. In what ways can we use money to be "rich toward God"?

13

Epistle Study/Pre-Paid Penalty

STEP ONE: Start with the OPEN questions on pages 11-12.

STEP TWO: Read James 5:1-6 and discuss the questions below with your group. If you do not understand a word or phrase, check the Reference Notes on page 15.

> *¹Now listen, you rich people, weep and wail because of the misery that is coming upon you. ²Your wealth has rotted, and moths have eaten your clothes. ³Your gold and silver are corroded. Their corrosion will testify against you and eat your flesh like fire. You have hoarded wealth in the last days. ⁴Look! The wages you failed to pay the workmen who mowed your fields are crying out against you. The cries of the harvesters have reached the ears of the Lord Almighty. ⁵You have lived on earth in luxury and self-indulgence. You have fattened yourselves in the day of slaughter. ⁶You have condemned and murdered innocent men who were opposing you.*
>
> ***James 5:1-6 NIV***

1. How do you feel reading this? What does this make you want to do?

2. Why is James so "down" on wealthy people?

3. From your personal observations, what does wealth usually do to people?

4. Is James condemning wealth or the abuse of wealth? How can one avoid abusing wealth?

5. How does God feel about the abuse of others through power and wealth?

6. How does God feel about the use of riches and money to live a life of luxury and self-indulgence?

7. What are the consequences for people who live life this way?

8. Taking James' teaching from head to heart, and from heart to pocketbook, what will you *do* with it?

REFLECT | **STEP THREE: As time allows, discuss with your group your agreement or disagreement with the following statements.**

- The constant desire to have still more things and a still better life and the struggle to obtain them imprints many Western faces with worry and even depression, though it is customary to conceal such feelings.

    — *Aleksandr Solzhenitsyn*

- Things are to be used and God is to be loved. We get into trouble when we begin to use God and love things.

    — *Jay Kesler*

APPLY | **STEP FOUR: By the standard of the rest of the world, most Americans are rich. Much responsibility comes with this privileged position. Answer the following questions and discuss your responses with your group.**

1. What are some of the "hidden" costs of pursuing more money and material possessions?

2. What are some of the rights which come with having adequate financial resources? What are some of the responsibilities?

3. In what practical ways do you think God would want you to use your financial resources more effectively?

REFERENCE NOTES | **Summary . . .** James is on the theme of wealth. He shows that riches are, indeed, a great burden when seen in eternal terms. In an unusually vivid passage, James points out the ultimate worthlessness of wealth in the face of the coming judgment. Although he is addressing the rich directly, he is also warning Christians not to covet wealth. Wealth is an illusion. It gives one a false sense of security. Not only that, it is gained at the expense of the poor, even to the extent of depriving them of their lives. All this to allow the rich to live in self-indulgent ways. In the previous passage James was concerned with the merchant class, business people who were, in this case, Christians (4:13–17). In this passage, his focus is on the landowner class who were, by and large, non-Christians.

v. 1 **Now listen . . .** James uses an impersonal mode of address.

rich people . . . In the first century there was a great gulf between rich and poor. Whereas a poor laborer (as in v. 4) might have received one denarius a day as wages (see Matt. 20:2, 9), a rich widow was said to have cursed the scribes because they allowed her only 400 gold denari a day to spend on luxuries! (Jeremias). In the face of such extravagance, the words of James take on new meaning. (See also Matt. 6:19-21, 24; Mark 10:17-31; Luke 6:24.)

Peter Davids argues that the people in view here are wealthy non-Christians since James seems to reserve the word *rich* for those outside the Christian community (see 1:10; 2:6).

weep . . . James says that the appropriate response for these wealthy non-Christians is tears. Their luxury is only for the moment. In contrast, in 1:2 and 12, he urged the poor Christians to rejoice because their present suffering will pass, bringing with it great reward.

wail . . . This is a strong word meaning "to shriek" or "howl," and is used to describe the terror that will be felt by the damned. (See Isa. 13:6; 14:31; Amos 8:3.)

the misery that is coming . . . James is referring to the future Day of Judgment, an event that will take place when the Lord returns. The noun *misery* is related (in the Greek) to the verb *grieve* used in 4:9. However, there is an important difference between the two uses. In 4:9 the grieving was self-imposed, the result of seeing one's failure, and it had a good result. Repentance opened up one to grace. But here this wretchedness results from the horror of being judged.

vv. 2-3 . . . James points to the three major forms of wealth in the first century: food, clothes, and precious metals, and describes the decay of each. Agricultural products like corn and oil will rot. Clothes will become moth-eaten. Even precious metal will corrode.

v. 2 **clothes** . . . Garments were one of the main forms of wealth in the first century. They were used as a means of payment, given as gifts, and passed on to one's children. (See Gen. 45:22; Josh. 7:21; Jdg. 14:12; 2 Kings 5:5; Acts 20:33.)

v. 3 **corroded** . . . Gold and silver do not, of course, rust or corrode (though silver will tarnish). James is using hyperbole to make his point: no form of wealth will make a person immune from the final judgment.

16

testify against you . . . The existence of rotten food, moth-eaten garments, and rusty coins will stand as a condemnation against the person. Instead of being stored, these goods should have been used to feed and clothe the poor.

eat your flesh like fire . . . In a striking image, James pictures wealth as having now turned against the person and become part of the torment he or she must endure. Just as rust eats through metal, so too it will eat through the flesh of the rich. (See Luke 16:19-31; Mark 9:43.)

the last days . . . The early Christians felt that Jesus would return very shortly, to draw his people to himself and to establish his kingdom on earth. James' point is: how inappropriate it is to give your energies over to accumulating treasures when, in effect, time itself is drawing to a close. This is an example of the kind of arrogance and pride that plans boldly for the future as if a person could control what lies ahead (see 4:14-16). "The rich gather and invest as if they or their descendants will live forever, yet the last days, the beginning of the end, are already here. James sees as tragic figures well-dressed men and women pondering investments over excellent meals; they act as if they were winners, but in reality have lost the only game that matters" (Davids, GNC).

vv. 4-6 . . . James now gets very specific as he details just how it is that these folks were able to accumulate such wealth. In particular he points to the injustices leveled against those who worked on the farms.

v. 4 **Look!** . . . James will not let them turn away from this stinging condemnation. They must see things as they are. They must face the reality of their own injustice.

wages you failed to pay . . . If a laborer was not given his wages at the end of the day, his family would go hungry the next day. The Old Testament insists that it is wrong to withhold wages. A worker was to be paid immediately. "Despite a host of Old Testament laws (Lev. 19:13; Deut. 24:14-15), ways were found to withhold payments (e.g., Jer. 22:13, Mal. 3:5). One might withhold them until the end of the harvest season to keep the worker coming back, grasp at a technicality to show that the contract was not fulfilled, or just be too tired to pay that night. If the poor worker complained, the landlord could blacklist him; if he went to court the rich had the better lawyers. James pictures the money in the pockets of the rich, money that should have been paid to the laborers, crying out for justice" (Davids, GNC).

the workmen . . . In Palestine, day laborers were used to plant and harvest the crops. They were cheaper than slaves, since if a slave converted to Judaism, he or she had to be freed in the sabbatical year.

fields . . . The Greek word means "estates." These were the large tracts of land owned by the very wealthy.

crying out . . . This is a word used to describe the wild, incoherent cry of an animal.

the Lord Almighty . . . Literally, "The Lord of Sabbath" or "Lord of Hosts," i.e., the commander of the heavenly armies. This is an unusual title, found at only one other place in the New Testament (and there it is a quote—Romans 9:29). James has probably drawn the title from Isaiah 5:7, 9, 16, 24—a chapter whose concerns parallel his own in this passage.

v. 5 **luxury** . . . In contrast to the hunger of the laborers is the soft living of the land owners (see Amos 6:1–7).

self-indulgence . . . "To live in lewdness and lasciviousness and wanton riotousness" (Barclay). Not just luxury but vice is in view here.

day of slaughter . . . Cattle were pampered and fattened for one purpose only: to be slaughtered. On the day when this took place a great feast was held.

v. 6 . . . There is yet another accusation against the rich—they use their wealth and power to oppress the poor even to the point of death. (See Amos 5:11f.; 8:4f.)

SESSION 3
Low Finance

The "flip side" of wealth is poverty. Even our wealthy nation has obvious evidences of poverty. As we drive through the ghettos and barrios of our major cities, we are painfully aware that not everyone lives as well as we As we walk the downtown streets of our glass and steel cities, we see th homeless scrounging through the trash baskets or sleeping on the sidev As we tour through the scenic countrysides of America, we are often startled by the unexpected sight of dilapidated houses and run-down towns.

The statistics give our senses no relief. There are about 35 million people in America's third world. Poor Americans are about equally divided between our cities and our rural areas. Interestingly, most poor people in the United States do not receive welfare payments. About 42% of all poor people over the age of 14 have jobs. The working poor have become one of the most overlooked and neglected groups in our society.

Many of us feel uncomfortably guilty when we see poor people or read about them. We may feel overwhelmed and helpless even when we have compassion. We are not helpless. There are many religious and charitable organizations through which we can express our concern. We can give our money and/or our time to help ease the suffering of less-fortunate people. Or we may want to "brainstorm" creative solutions which may give opportunities to people with little hope.

Jesus understood that poverty is not a vice, but he also understood that it is not a virtue. In the following Gospel passage, Jesus puts wealth and poverty into a spiritual perspective. He shows that giving to God produces true wealth. In the Epistle Study, the Apostle Paul praises the generous spirit. He teaches us the paradox that out of poverty comes wealth.

LEADER:
IF YOU HAVE
RE THAN SEVEN
T THE MEETING,
SUBDIVIDE
ITO GROUPS OF
FOUR FOR
GREATER
PARTICIPATION
(SEE BOX ON
PAGE 6).

OPTION 1

OPEN

Gospel Study/Small Change

STEP ONE: Answer the following question and share your response with your group.

If you had the power to alleviate poverty, what would you do?
_____ I would make the poor all rich
_____ I would give them all jobs
_____ I would put them all on welfare
_____ I would see that they all got an education
_____ I would see that they all had enough to eat

_____ Nothing, we will always have poor people
_____ I would teach them to help themselves
_____ I would address the "economic violence" which keeps people trapped in poverty

STUDY

STEP TWO: Read Mark 12:41-44 and discuss your responses to the following questions with your group.

> *41Jesus sat down opposite the place where the offerings were put and watched the crowd putting their money into the temple treasury. Many rich people threw in large amounts. 42But a poor widow came and put in two small copper coins, worth only a fraction of a penny.*
> *43Calling his disciples to him, Jesus said, "I tell you the truth, this poor widow has put more into the treasury than all the others. 44They all gave out of their wealth; but she, out of her poverty, put in everything—all she had to live on."*
>
> *Mark 12:41-44 NIV*

1. What do you usually feel or do when an offering plate is passed?
   a. I feel guilty if I don't put something in
   b. I feel proud if I do put something in
   c. I reach for the $5 bill; if I only have a $20 bill, I pass
   d. I give what pocket change I have leftover
   e. I give whatever I have on me, knowing I'll be blessed later

2. Why do you think Jesus was watching people give to the temple treasury?
   a. He was just "killing time"
   b. He was rating the givers
   c. He was curious
   d. He was setting up a teaching situation for his disciples

3. In your opinion, why do you think most people give money to churches?
   a. They are trying to buy their way into heaven
   b. They want to keep the institutional church going
   c. They want to contribute to the ministry of the church
   d. They feel guilty if they don't give
   e. They want a tax deduction

4. What do you think motivated the widow to give all she had?
   a. She was possibly mentally-deranged
   b. She loved God very deeply
   c. She was thankful for what she had
   d. She believed that it would help her get to heaven

5. What was Jesus trying to teach his disciples?
   a. That poor people are better than rich people
   b. That everyone should give to God
   c. That we should give our all to God
   d. That giving should be sacrifical
   e. That we should give until it "hurts"

6. What is your opinion of the widow's actions?
   a. Her actions were admirable, but I wouldn't do it
   b. She was foolhardy and not using common sense
   c. She was doing exactly what God wanted her to do
   d. She should have talked to a financial planner

7. What do you think these verses are trying to teach you?
   a. That you should be completely "sold-out" to God
   b. Attitude, not amount, is all that matters
   c. That you can give to God no matter how rich or poor you are
   d. That you do not need a big bank balance to give
   e. It's not how much you give, but how much is left over, that counts with God.

APPLY

STEP THREE: Answer the following questions and share your responses with your group.

1. Have you ever been in a situation where you gave sacrificially? What were the circumstances?

2. How did you feel?

3. What opportunities do you now have to give to God and others sacrificially?

OPTION 2

Epistle Study/Earnest Money

OPEN

STEP ONE: Start with the OPEN question on pages 19-20.

STUDY

STEP TWO: Read 2 Corinthians 8:1-15 and discuss your responses to the following questions with your group. If you do not understand a word or phrase, check the Reference Notes on page 23.

¹And now, brothers, we want you to know about the grace that God has given the Macedonian churches. ²Out of the most severe trial, their overflowing joy and their extreme poverty welled up in rich generosity. ³For I testify that they gave as much as they were able, and even beyond their ability. Entirely on their own, ⁴they urgently pleaded with us for the privilege of sharing in this service to the saints. ⁵And they did not do as we expected, but they gave themselves first to the Lord and then to us in keeping with God's will.

⁶*So we urged Titus, since he had earlier made a beginning, to bring also to completion this act of grace on your part. ⁷But just as you excel in everything—in faith, in speech, in knowledge, in complete earnestness and in your love for us—see that you also excel in this grace of giving.*

⁸*I am not commanding you, but I want to test the sincerity of your love by comparing it with the earnestness of others. ⁹For you know the grace of our Lord Jesus Christ, that though he was rich, yet for your sakes he became poor, so that you through his poverty might become rich.*

¹⁰*And here is my advice about what is best for you in this matter: Last year you were the first not only to give but also to have the desire to do so. ¹¹Now finish the work, so that your eager willingness to do it may be matched by your completion of it, according to your means. ¹²For if the willingness is there, the gift is acceptable according to what one has, not according to what he does not have.*

¹³*Our desire is not that others might be relieved while you are hard pressed, but that there might be equality. ¹⁴At the present time your plenty will supply what they need. Then there will be equality, ¹⁵as it is written: "He who gathered much did not have too much, and he who gathered little did not have too little."*

2 Corinthians 8:1-15 NIV

1. What were you doing last year at this time that still needs to be completed? What project are you doing now that will take another year to complete?

2. While we live with undone work, Paul is emphasizing unexpected grace. What exactly is this "grace" that Paul wants the Corinthians and us to know about?

3. How can "overflowing joy" be present during "the most severe trials"?

4. How can "rich generosity" be present with "extreme poverty"?

5. How would you describe the giving habits of the Macedonian churches? Of your church?

6. What was their priority in giving?

7. Why did Christ choose a life of poverty?

8. What is Paul's advice to the Corinthians concerning the giving project they had begun the year before?

9. According to these verses, what should be the relationship between "haves" and "have-nots" in the Christian community?

STEP THREE: As time allows, discuss with your group your agreement or disagreement with the following statements.

- Find out how much God has given you and from it take what you need; the remainder which you do not require is needed by others.
  — Augustine

- To feel sorry for the needy is not the mark of a Christian—to help them is.
  — Frank A. Clark

STEP FOUR: Answer the following questions and share your responses with your group.

1. What are some evidences of poverty in your community?

2. What attitude does God want you to have toward the poor?

3. What can you and your group do to help meet the needs of poor people in your community?

Summary . . . Here Paul discusses the Corinthian collection to be taken up on behalf of the poor in Jerusalem (Acts 24:17). Having been charged by the "pillars" of the Jerusalem church "to remember the poor" (Gal. 2:10), Paul did so with his characteristic gusto. Though he had sent detailed instructions to the Corinthians concerning this collection (1 Cor. 16:1-4), he did not himself collect their gifts during his second, difficult visit. Instead, he asked Titus to attend to this when he returned carrying his "severe letter," but again this proved impossible. So here Paul sets out his new plan: Titus and two companions will collect the gifts. As it turned out, this plan also came unstuck due to the troubles discussed in 2 Corinthians 10-13. In fact, Paul himself probably picked up the collection during a three-month visit to Greece (Acts 20:1-3). In Romans 15:26, which he wrote at Corinth, he mentions this collection (Corinth was located in Achaia).

Though the Gentile churches were not themselves wealthy (1 Cor. 1:26; 2 Cor. 8:2), they were better off than the poor in Jerusalem. By sharing in this way the Gentiles were able to show their gratitude to Israel for the gift of the gospel. This was a very significant gesture, since conservative Jewish Christians were highly suspect of the Gentile churches founded by Paul. In fact, some of them visited these churches and told the Gentile Christians that they must keep the law of Moses to be true Christians (prompting Paul's fiery letter to the Galatians). The collection could heal these wounds.

v. 1 **And now . . .** Paul has just expressed his *complete confidence* (7:16) in the Corinthians, and in the light of this, he broaches the subject of the collection.

the grace . . . Though they were themselves poor, in response to God's gift of grace to them and as a result of the spirit of generosity given them by God's grace, they share what they have with the poor in Jerusalem.

Macedonian churches . . . Macedonia was the Roman province just north of Achaia (where Corinth was located). The churches were probably located at least in Philippi, Thessalonica, and Berea (Acts 16:11–17:15).

v. 2 **severe trial . . .** In particular, the church at Thessalonica seems to have been subjected to extensive persecution because of its faith. (See 1 Thess. 1:6–8; 2:14; 3:3–5; 2 Thess. 1:4–10; Phil. 1:29–30.)

extreme poverty . . . Macedonia itself was a rich province with a flourishing mining (gold, silver, copper), lumber, and agricultural industry. The Christians, it seems, were poor, due perhaps to the persecution. Christians may have been fired from jobs or their businesses boycotted. Note the marvelous equation: Severe trial plus extreme poverty plus joy equal great generosity.

vv. 3–4 . . . Despite their own poverty, they begged to be allowed to give generously to their Christian brothers and sisters in Jerusalem.

v. 5 . . . The Macedonians saw their giving as an act of devotion—both to the Lord and to Paul. They did not limit their giving to money but gave of themselves.

v. 6 **earlier made a beginning . . .** Titus probably had attempted to take up the collection when he was in Corinth in order to deliver the "severe" letter. Paul wants him to finish this job.

v. 7 . . . Paul exhorts the Corinthians to participate in giving as wholeheartedly as they participate in the exercise of other spiritual gifts. This is the ideal way to appeal to them since as is evident from 1 Corinthians, they prided themselves on such spiritual gifts and allowed them to flourish in their midst (although they were preoccupied with certain gifts).

vv. 8-9 . . . Paul gives a twofold example by which the Corinthians may measure the extent of their love—that of the Macedonians and that of the Lord.

v. 9 **he became poor . . .** The Lord left all ᴜᵢe riches and benefits of heaven to be born of a woman (Gal. 4:4), to live a difficult life (Matt. 8:20), and then to die (Phil. 2:6-11). He is the ultimate model of giving.

you . . . might become rich . . . Had not Christ left heaven, the Corinthians would never have known the riches of salvation.

vv. 10-11 . . . Paul has already given three reasons why they ought to participate in the collection: the needs of the people in Jerusalem, the example of the Macedonians, and the example of the Lord. Now he adds a fourth: they ought to complete what they started.

v. 12 . . . The question is not how much or how little one gives, only that one is willing to do so—presumably motivated by one's love for God and for people.

vv. 13-14 **equality . . .** The idea is *not* that by means of the collection the saints in Jerusalem would become rich while the Corinthians would be reduced to poverty. The idea is *equality*: that in their abundance the Corinthians share what they have with those who are in need. Likewise, in the future, it could be the other way around and the Corinthians could expect aid if they needed it from Christians in Jerusalem and elsewhere.

v. 15 . . . Paul demonstrates this principle from Scripture, pointing to the experience of the Israelites in the wilderness when collecting manna. Equality was the watchword, with none having too much or too little.

SESSION 4
Belly Up

Most of us have lived long enough to regret our use and abuse of money. Perhaps we have invested our hard-earned money in a "sure-thing" investment only to watch it evaporate. Maybe unemployment dried up our savings leaving us to struggle back to financial stability. Obviously, there are many ways to go "belly up." Losing our money and assets can be a very traumatic experience. It makes us feel vulnerable and exposed.

It is often at these times of financial failure that we get a better perspective of reality. When the security and insulation of money is withdrawn, we cannot help but recognize our defenselessness. Often we turn to God in our moment of weakness and then forget about him when financial security returns.

In the following Gospel Study, we see a young man who is stripped of his fortune and financial security. It causes him to come to his senses and to experience the forgiveness of his father. In the Epistle passage, Paul also warns us of the allure and danger of money.

OPTION 1

Gospel Study/Debt to Society

OPEN

STEP ONE: Answer the following question and share your response with your group.

Which of the following situations make you feel most financially insecure? (choose two)

LEADER: IF YOU HAVE MORE THAN SEVEN AT THE MEETING, SUBDIVIDE INTO GROUPS OF FOUR FOR GREATER PARTICIPATION (SEE BOX ON PAGE 6).

- ____ paying for a college education
- ____ putting food on the table
- ____ keeping my job
- ____ paying the mortgage
- ____ soaring medical bills
- ____ making my car payment
- ____ paying off my credit cards
- ____ keeping my business going
- ____ being sued
- ____ preparing for retirement
- ____ paying taxes
- ____ being robbed
- ____ keeping up with inflation

STUDY | **STEP TWO: Read Luke 15:11-32** and discuss your responses to the following questions with your group.

> *11Jesus continued: There was a man who had two sons. 12The younger one said to his father, 'Father, give me my share of the estate.' So he divided his property between them.*
>
> *13"Not long after that, the younger son got together all he had, set off for a distant country and there squandered his wealth in wild living. 14After he had spent everything, there was a severe famine in that whole country, and he began to be in need. 15So he went and hired himself out to a citizen of that country, who sent him to his fields to feed pigs. 16He longed to fill his stomach with the pods that the pigs were eating, but no one give him anything.*
>
> *17"When he came to his senses, he said, 'How many of my father's hired men have food to spare, and here I am starving to death! 18I will set out and go back to my father and say to him: Father, I have sinned against heaven and against you. 19I am no longer worthy to be called your son; make me like one of your hired men.' 20So he got up and went to his father.*
>
> *"But while he was still a long way off, his father saw him and was filled with compassion for him; he ran to his son, threw his arms around him and kissed him.*
>
> *21"The son said to him, 'Father, I have sinned against heaven and against you. I am no longer worthy to be called your son.'*
>
> *22"But the father said to his servants, 'Quick! Bring the best robe and put it on him. Put a ring on his finger and sandals on his feet. 23Bring the fattened calf and kill it. Let's have a feast and celebrate. 24For this son of mine was dead and is alive again; he was lost and is found.' So they began to celebrate.*
>
> *25"Meanwhile, the older son was in the field. When he came near the house, he heard the music and dancing. 26So he called one of the servants and asked him what was going on. 27'Your brother has come,' he replied, 'and your father has killed a fattened calf because he has him back safe and sound.'*
>
> *28"The older brother became angry and refused to go in. So his father went out and pleaded with him. 29But he answered his father, 'Look! All these years I have been slaving for you and never disobeyed your orders. Yet you never gave me even a young goat so I could celebrate with my friends. 30But when this son of yours who has squandered your property with prostitutes comes home, you kill the fattened calf for him!'*
>
> *31" 'My son,' the father said, 'you are always with me, and everything I have is yours. 32But we have to celebrate and be glad, because this brother of yours was dead and is alive again; he was lost and is found.' "*
>
> *Luke 15:11-32 NIV*

1. If you were to project yourself into this story, with which character do you most readily identify? And why?
   a. The younger son, because I used to squander my allowance and even sowed a few wild oats
   b. The first born, because I resented younger siblings getting privileges that I didn't
   c. The waiting father, because my kids keep me up
   d. The narrator, because I feel like a spectator watching what God is doing in the lives of others
   e. The son who experienced grace despite doing bad
   f. The son who felt bound by his having to be good
   g. The pigs, whose company helps the prodigal realize he's hit bottom

2. Why do you think the younger son wanted his share of the estate?
   a. He wanted to see the world
   b. He wanted to get away from home
   c. He wanted to "sow his wild oats"
   d. He wanted to seek his fortune

3. Why do you think his father let him go so easily?
   a. He was tired of fighting with his son
   b. He identified with his son's desire to leave
   c. He knew it was necessary for his son to learn the hard way
   d. It really wasn't easy for him to see his son go

4. Why do you think the son squandered his money so quickly?
   a. He had no experience in managing money
   b. He was raised as a spoiled kid
   c. He didn't earn the money, so "easy come, easy go"
   d. He thought it would never run out
   e. He was having too good a time to care

5. What is your attitude toward his actions?
   a. He was foolish and deserved what he got
   b. I wish someone had given him advice first
   c. He is to be pitied
   d. Everyone goes through a similar experience sooner or later

6. What is often learned through the experience of "hitting the bottom"?
   a. You learn that you can fail
   b. You learn that you are not "infallible"
   c. You learn that you cannot control all of life's circumstances
   d. You learn that you are capable of poor judgment
   e. You learn that emotions can control your life

7. What do you think Jesus is teaching through this parable?
   a. That squandering money is a foolish thing to do
   b. That money should not come between father and son
   c. That forgiveness is an act of love
   d. That genuine repentance leads to a changed life
   e. That sinful living will get you in trouble

APPLY

STEP THREE: Answer the following questions and share your responses with your group.

1. Have you ever squandered a significant amount of money? How did it make you feel?

2. If you could do it over again, what would you do differently?

3. Have you ever "hit the bottom"? What did you learn from that experience?

OPTION 2

Epistle Study/Counterfeit Money

OPEN

STEP ONE: Start with the OPEN question on page 26.

STUDY

STEP TWO: Read 1 Timothy 6:3-10 and discuss your responses to the following questions with your group. If you do not understand a word or phrase, check the Reference Notes on page 31.

³If anyone teaches false doctrine and does not agree to the sound instruction of our Lord Jesus Christ and to godly teaching, ⁴he is conceited and understands nothing. He has an unhealthy interest in controversies and quarrels about words that result in envy, strife, malicious talk, evil suspicions ⁵and constant friction between men of corrupt mind, who have been robbed of the truth and who think that godliness is a means to financial gain.
⁶But godliness with contentment is great gain. ⁷For we brought nothing into the world, and we can take nothing out of it. ⁸But if we have food and clothing, we will be content with that. ⁹People who want to be rich fall into temptation and a trap and into many foolish and harmful desires that plunges men into ruin and destruction. ¹⁰For the love of money is the root of all kinds of evil. Some people, eager for money, have wandered from the faith and pierced themselves with many griefs.

1 Timothy 6:3-10 NIV

1. What ad slogan or literary title best captures your view of money?
   a. "Money (That's What I Want)"—the Beatles
   b. "Money Can't Buy Me Love"—the Beatles
   c. "You Can't Take It With You"—Moss Hart and George S. Kaufman
   d. "You Can Have It All"—beer commercial
   e. "I Can't Help Myself"—the Four Tops

2. What "false doctrines" about money are taught and believed by your contemporaries?

3. In what ways does/has money corrupted Christians?

4. What is the difference between "godliness with contentment" and "godliness as a means to financial gain"?

5. If we "can't take it with us," what should we do with money?

6. Why is the pursuit of wealth a trap?

7. How does "the love of money" affect our relationship with God?

8. What is a spiritually healthy attitude toward money?

REFLECT

STEP THREE: As time allows, discuss with your group your agreement or disagreement with the following statements.

- When I have money, I get rid of it quickly, lest it find a way into my heart.
  — *John Wesley*

- Jesus taught that money is one of the spiritual powers we fight—not simply green paper or copper-nickel sandwiches. Money is not some thing; it is someone. And as someone, it tricks us into thinking we master it, when inevitably it masters us.
  — *David Neff*

APPLY

STEP FOUR: Answer the following questions and share your responses with your group.

1. What are some examples of how "the love of money is the root of all evil"?

2. If you were to put it into words, what do you think God wants you to do with your money?

Summary . . . In this unit Paul summarizes the problem of false teachers and Timothy's role in dealing with them. In the process he provides some more details about the false teachers. It turns out that what motivates them is pride, a love of argument, and greed (vv. 3–5). However, what really ought to motivate us, Paul says, is "godliness with contentment" (vv. 6–10).

> vv. 3–5 . . . False doctrine, Paul says, brings negative results. Those who have departed from the teaching of Jesus are people of dubious character who have brought disharmony into the church.

> v. 3 **false doctrine** . . . Paul began this letter by pointing out that the problem in Ephesus was "false doctrine" (1:3). He now returns to this theme as he draws his letter to a close.

> **the sound instruction of our Lord Jesus Christ** . . . This is their error. They have departed from the teaching of Jesus. This statement seems to indicate that early in the life of the church the teachings of Jesus were collected and taught. The first Gospels were probably written around the time of this letter. However, whether this phrase refers to a written source or not, the point is that the origin of "sound instruction" is the Lord Jesus Christ (see also 1:10, 4:6).

> v. 4 **he is conceited and understands nothing** . . . This is the first thing Paul says about these teachers. They are swollen with pride when, in fact, they are really quite ignorant. The NEB puts it well: they are "pompous ignoramus[es]"!

> **unhealthy interest** . . . This is literally "being sick or diseased." This sort of "morbid craving" (as Bauer defines it) stands in sharp contrast to the sound (or "healthy") instruction of verse 3.

> **controversies** . . . This is more than just "disputes." The word refers to a sort of idle speculation. They were preoccupied "with pseudo-intellectual theorizings" (Kelly).

> **quarrels** . . . This is literally a "battle of words," which Paul sharply criticizes. He "paints in lurid colours the pride from which it springs, the spirit of anti-social bitterness and suspicion which it sows in the church, and the moral degeneracy which it eventually produces. The picture is a savage one, and although some of the details may be borrowed from conventional catalogues of vices, it suggests a concrete situation which excited Paul's distress and indignation" (Kelly).

result in . . . Paul identifies two negative results of this sick preoccupation with word battles. First, it produces strife within the church and second, it brings about a kind of corruption or decay to the minds of the teachers themselves.

envy . . . Controversy produces jealousy as people pick sides (see Gal. 5:21; Rom. 1:29 where envy is said to be one of the fruits of the sinful nature).

malicious talk, evil suspicions . . . This quarreling drives people to insult and question one another.

v. 5 **corrupt mind . . .** *Mind* refers not just to "the power of reason" but to one's whole way of thinking.

robbed of the truth . . . Such corruption results in the loss of the very truth of the gospel.

godliness is a means to financial gain . . . As Paul has hinted in 3:3 and 8, the bottom line motivation of these false teachers is the money they make from their teaching. Paul does not consider it wrong for a person to be paid for teaching (see 5:17–18) but he is incensed when greed is the main motivation for ministry.

vv. 6–10 **. . .** Paul picks up on this problem of greed and says two things about it. First, godliness is to be much preferred to profit (vv. 6–8), and second, a love of money brings dire results.

v. 6 **. . . .** "This verse stands in immediate contrast to the last words in verse 5, with a striking play on terms. *They* think godliness 'is a way to become rich.' Well (Gk., *de*, "indeed"), they are right. There *is* great profit (now used metaphorically) in godliness (*religion does make a person very rich*), provided it is accompanied by a 'contented spirit' (Moffatt, Kelly), that is, if one is satisfied with what one has and does not seek material gain" (Fee).

contentment . . . This was a favorite word of the Stoic philosophers from whom Paul borrowed it. (Zeno, the founder of this philosophical school came from Tarsus, Paul's hometown.) This word refers to a person who is not impacted by circumstances. Such a person is self-contained and thus able to rise above all conditions. For Paul, however, this sort of contentment was derived from the Lord (see Phil. 4:11).

vv. 7–8 . . . There are two reasons why "godliness with contentment" brings great gain. First, at death people can take nothing with them, so why worry about material gain that has to be given up in the end anyway? Second, if people have the essentials in life, this should be enough.

vv. 9–10 . . . Paul ends by pointing out the dangers of riches. In these verses he chronicles the downward process that begins with the desire "to get rich." Such a desire leads into "temptation" which is, in turn, "a trap." The "trap" is the "many foolish and harmful desires" that afflict the greedy person. The end result is that such people are "plunge[d] . . . into ruin and destruction."

v. 9 **temptation** . . . Greed causes people to notice and desire what they might not otherwise have paid attention to.

v. 10 **For the love of money is a root of all kinds of evil** . . . Paul is probably quoting a well-known proverb in order to support the assertion he makes in verse 9 that the desire for money leads to ruin. This verse is often misquoted as "money is the root of all evil." While Paul clearly sees the danger of money, he is not contending that *all* evil can be traced to avarice.

some people . . . have wandered . . . Here is the problem. Some of the false teachers have given in to the temptation to riches. They were probably once good leaders in the church but they got caught by Satan (4:1–2), became enamored with speculative ideas (6:3–5), and in the end were pulled down by their love for money.

SESSION 5
Good Investment

Do you ever dream of making that one super investment that will set you up for life? Perhaps it is starting a business which "can't miss." Or investing in a hot over-the-counter stock which will bring you your bonanza. Maybe you think that you have an excellent chance of winning the lottery or hitting the jackpot. Or perhaps amassing a real estate empire is the way to go.

Investments have a certain allure for many of us. They promise the opportunity of making more money while working less. Obviously, some investments are good and some are not so good; and some investments are riskier than others.

Jesus recognized the importance of investing. In the following parable, he addressed the investment of our lives as well as our money. In the end, it is the investment of·our lives—our time and our energy—which is most important. In the Epistle Study, Paul exemplifies "life investment." He had learned to be content with whatever he had, be it a little or a lot.

OPTION 1

Gospel Study/Investment and Return

OPEN

STEP ONE: In which of the following are you most likely to invest your money and time? Why?

____ a passbook savings account
____ a charitable organization
____ a certificate of deposit
____ your church or other religious organization
____ stocks and bonds
____ other people
____ commodity futures market
____ helping others
____ a money market account
____ a political organization
____ U.S. savings bonds
____ environmental causes
____ a life insurance policy
____ your child's education
____ gold
____ your marriage
____ Ginnie, Fannie, or Freddie
____ your family

**LEADER:
IF YOU HAVE
MORE THAN SEVEN
AT THE MEETING,
SUBDIVIDE
INTO GROUPS OF
FOUR FOR
GREATER
PARTICIPATION
(SEE BOX ON
PAGE 6).**

STUDY | STEP TWO: Read Matthew 25:14-30 and discuss your responses to the following questions with your group.

14"Again, it will be like a man going on a journey, who called his servants and entrusted his property to them. 15To one he gave five talents of money, to another two talents, and to another one talent, each according to his ability. Then he went on his journey. 16The man who had received the five talents went at once and put his money to work and gained five more. 17So also, the one with two talents gained two more. 18But the man who had received the one talent went off, dug a hole in the ground and hid his master's money.

19"After a long time the master of those servants returned and settled accounts with them. 20The man who had received the five talents brought the other five. 'Master,' he said, 'you entrusted me with five talents. See, I have gained five more.'

21"His master replied, 'Well done good and faithful servant! You have been faithful with a few things; I will put you in charge of many things. Come and share your master's happiness'!

22"The man with two talents also came. 'Master,' he said, 'you entrusted me with two talents; see, I have gained two more.'

23"His master replied, 'Well done, good and faithful servant! You have been faithful with a few things; I will put you in charge of many things. Come and share your master's happiness!'

24"Then the man who had received the one talent came. 'Master,' he said, 'I knew that you are a hard man, harvesting where you have not sown and gathering where you have not scattered seeds. 25So I was afraid and went out and hid your talent in the ground. See, here is what belongs to you.'

26"His master replied, 'You wicked, lazy servant! So you knew that I harvest where I have not sown and gather where I have not scattered seed? 27Well then, you should have put my money on deposit with the bankers, so that when I returned I would have received it back with interest.

28" 'Take the talent from him and give it to the one who had the ten talents. 29For everyone who has will be given more, and he will have an abundance. Whoever does not have, even what he has will be taken from him. 30And throw that worthless servant outside, into the darkness, where there will be weeping and gnashing of teeth.' "

Matthew 25:14-30 NIV

1. What were you known for in school—what talents did others recognize in you?

2. In this parable, with which one of the following characters do you identify?
   a. The first servant/5 talents
   b. The second servant/2 talents
   c. The third servant/1 talent
   d. The master
   e. None of the characters

3. Why did the master entrust his money and property to his servants?
   a. In his absence, they were his representatives
   b. He needed a vacation
   c. He was testing their commitment to him
   d. He wanted to make more money
   e. He trusted and had faith in them

4. Why did he give an unequal amount of talents/money to the three servants?
   a. Because he was "playing favorites"
   b. Because he knew they had different capabilities
   c. Because he was running out of money
   d. Because he did not want to waste money on a scoundrel

5. What is your opinion of the master after he "settled accounts" with his servants?
   a. He was being quite fair
   b. He showed himself to be a shrewd businessman
   c. He was being unfair
   d. He was a "tough cookie"
   e. He was a teacher handing out "test grades"

6. Why did the master respond the same way to the first two servants?
   a. He favored them over the third servant
   b. He appreciated their loyalty and commitment
   c. He had a poor relationship with the third servant
   d. He was more concerned with the quality of their response than the quantity of their response

7. Why did the third servant bury his money?
   a. He was afraid of the master
   b. He didn't think the master deserved any more money
   c. He resented the way the master made his money
   d. He was lazy

8. What is Jesus teaching you in this parable?
   a. That making money without working is important
   b. That investing in God's kingdom is very important
   c. That he has given Christians a "job" to do until his return
   d. That the rich will get richer
   e. That we better be ready when he returns
   f. That we should invest our "talents" in God's kingdom
   g. That God cannot tolerate laziness
   h. That judgment is coming for those who do not invest their lives wisely

APPLY

STEP THREE: Answer the following questions and share your responses with your group.

1. Which one of the following statements best describes how you feel about the way you are currently "investing" your life?
   _____ I am quite satisfied
   _____ I would like to make some changes
   _____ I need to change, but don't know what to do
   _____ I don't know what it means to "invest" my life
   _____ I haven't done a very good job of investing my life in anything worthwhile

2. What changes would be necessary to make you more satisfied with your life's investment?

OPTION 2

Epistle Study/Full Payment

OPEN

STEP ONE: Start with the OPEN question on page 34.

STUDY

STEP TWO: Read Philippians 4:10-20 and discuss the following questions with your group. If you do not understand a word or phrase, check the Reference Notes on page 39.

> *¹⁰I rejoice greatly in the Lord that at last you have renewed your concern for me. Indeed, you have been concerned, but you had no opportunity to show it. ¹¹I am not saying this because I am in need, for I have learned to be content whatever the circumstances. ¹²I know what it is to be in need, and I know what it is to have plenty. I have learned the secret of being content in any and every situation, whether well fed or hungry, whether living in plenty or in want. ¹³I can do everything through him who gives me strength.*

¹⁴Yet it was good of you to share in my troubles. ¹⁵Moreover, as you Philippians know, in the early days of your acquaintance with the gospel, when I set out from Macedonia, not one church shared with me in the matter of giving and receiving, except you only; ¹⁶for even when I was in Thessalonica, you sent me aid again and again when I was in need. ¹⁷Not that I am looking for a gift, but I am looking for what may be credited to your account. ¹⁸I have received full payment and even more; I am amply supplied, now that I have received from Epaphroditus the gifts you sent. They are a fragrant offering, an acceptable sacrifice, pleasing to God. ¹⁹And my God will meet all your needs according to his glorious riches in Christ Jesus.

²⁰To our God and Father be glory for ever and ever. Amen.

Philippians 4:10-20 NIV

1. What do you recall as the happiest or most carefree days of your life? Why do you look back on them with such fondness?

2. What is the apostle Paul's attitude in these verses?

3. What is Paul's perspective on "feast and famine"?

4. Why is he so confident about his ability to accept whatever happens to him?

5. Why is it good for the Philippian Christians to share in Paul's troubles?

6. What teachings on Christian community do you see here?

7. In what practical ways did/can the Philippian Christians invest in Paul's ministry?

8. In what practical ways can we likewise invest in Christian ministry?

REFLECT

STEP THREE: As time allows, discuss with your group your agreement or disagreement with the following statements.

- I fail or succeed in my stewardship of life in proportion to how convinced I am that life belongs to God.

  — Pearl Bartel

- Give according to your income lest God make your income according to your giving.

  — Peter Marshall

STEP FOUR: Answer the following questions and share your responses with your group.

1. What do you find most difficult about sharing your money?

2. What do you think God expects of you in regard to sharing your money?

Summary . . . Paul has completed the body of his letter. He has said all that needs to be said. What remains now is for him to finish off his letter with a few "housekeeping" comments. Specifically, he thanks the Philippians for their gift—albeit in a rather curious fashion (vv. 10–20) and then he passes along greetings from various people (vv. 21–23).

vv. 10-19 . . . It is difficult for Paul to know how to thank the Philippians properly for the gift they sent him via Epaphroditus. The problem is this. While he affirmed the right of an apostle to be supported by the church, he personally refused to accept such gifts, preferring to underwrite his own ministry by working as a tentmaker (Acts 18:3, 1 Thess. 2:5-12; 2 Thess. 3:7-12). As he explains elsewhere (1 Cor. 9:1-23) he did this so that no one could ever accuse him of preaching the gospel in order to make money, or say that the gospel was anything but a free gift from God. But the Philippians have sent him a gift—and this is not the first time. And while he is genuinely grateful, he also wants to assert his independence. So, his problem is how to thank them while simultaneously asking them not to send any more money. In these verses he manages this difficult balancing act with grace and skill.

v. 10 **I rejoice greatly . . .** This is the closest Paul gets to saying "thank you" to the Philippians. In this section about thanks he does not once use the word "thanks"! Still, this is not an insincere expression on Paul's part. He says that he rejoices *greatly* over what they have done. This is the only time in his letters that Paul ever adds a qualifier to "rejoicing," thus emphasizing the depth of his feeling toward the Philippians.

in the Lord . . . This is the fourth time that Paul has used this phrase in this chapter (4:1-2, 4, 10—see also 4:19).

that . . . you have been concerned . . . The cause of his rejoicing is not the gift, *per se*, but the concern that it evidenced.

at last . . . Apparently the Philippians had not been in contact with Paul for quite some time. The reason for this is not explained. However, the arrival of Epaphroditus renewed their contact with Paul for which he is grateful.

renewed . . . This is a rare Greek word which appears only at this place in the New Testament. It describes the flowering of a bush or tree and can be translated "blossomed." Paul is so grateful for their renewed care after this long silence that to him it is like seeing a shoot sprout out of the ground and burst into blossom.

Indeed, you have been concerned . . . Paul is not criticizing them for not being in touch. It is not that they did not want to come to his aid. They simply had no opportunity.

v. 11 . . . Having expressed his pleasure at this sign of their care, he then goes on to say: "But, in fact, I really did not need what you gave me!" This is the first of several alternations between commending them for their gift (vv. 10, 14-16, 18-20) and insisting on his right to self-sufficiency (vv. 11-13, 17).

need . . . This is another rare word, used only here and in Mark 12:44. It means "poverty" or "lack." Paul was not in difficult straits financially. He accepts their gift only because it is of great benefit *to them* to give in this way (see vv. 17-18).

content . . . Yet another rare word. This is its only appearance in the New Testament. Paul borrows it from the vocabulary of the Stoic philosophers for whom it was a favorite word. It was used to describe the person who was self-sufficient and able to exist without anything or anyone. Paul would have been familiar with stoicism since Zeno, the founder of this philosophical school, came from Tarsus, Paul's hometown. However, the sufficiency to which Paul refers is quite different from that of the philosophers. Paul's sufficiency is found in the Lord.

vv. 12-13 . . . Paul explains what he means by saying that he has learned to be content in all circumstances.

v. 12 **need** . . . This is a different Greek word from that translated "need" in verse 11. This word refers to the lowering of water in a river. As such, it is a reference to fundamental needs which are basic to life such as food and water. Paul has learned to exist even in the midst of abject poverty.

plenty . . . This is the opposite state to "need." It means literally, "to overflow," that is, to have enough for one's own daily needs plus something left over. In Luke 9:17 this same word is used to describe the food left over after Jesus fed the 5000. Although the root idea is not that of opulent luxury, the word came to mean extreme riches. In this verse Paul is contrasting two extremes: *deprivation,* when one lacks even the basic necessities of life, and *riches*, when one has far more than what one could possibly use.

I have learned the secret . . . This is the only occurrence of this verb in the New Testament. It is drawn from the world of the mystery religions and in that context would refer to the rites by which the initiate comes to understand the secret of the cult.

well fed . . . This is a word which describes force-fed animals who are stuffed to overflowing in order to fatten them for slaughter. It is used by Paul to define one of the extremes: having more than enough to eat.

hungry . . . This is the opposite condition. It refers to the absence of food (as against the abundance of food given the force-fed animals).

living in plenty or in want . . . Another set of contrasting words. It is by the experience of these extremes that Paul has come to know the secret of coping with all circumstances.

v. 13 **everything** . . . A better translation of this word would be "all these things." Paul is referring to what he has just described: his ability to exist in all types of material circumstances—wealth or poverty, abundant food or no food, etc. He is not suddenly making a general statement about his ability to do *anything.*

through him who gives me strength . . . The source of Paul's ability to exist successfully in all circumstances is his union with Christ. This is his "secret." While it is true that by going through a variety of difficult circumstances he has learned the discipline necessary to cope with hardship and abundance, it is also true that this ability is not merely self-generated. It comes from Christ. This is an illustration on an individual level of 2:12-13. Paul is working out his own salvation ("health," "wholeness") while simultaneously, God is working in him. See also 2 Corinthians 12:9-10.

v. 14 . . . Paul shifts from the issue of his self-sufficiency back to their act of generosity. They did a really beautiful thing (the root idea behind the word translated "good") by becoming partners in his hardships. See 1:5, 7 for this same note of partnership.

vv. 15-16 . . . See Acts 16:11-17:9 for an account of Paul's experience in Philippi and Thessalonica.

v. 16 **again and again** . . . This is one of the few churches from which Paul has accepted multiple gifts—which is an indicator of the special relationship he has with the Philippians.

vv. 17-18 . . . In these verses Paul uses a series of terms drawn from the world of commerce. "Looking for a gift" is "a technical term for the demand for payment of interest" (Gnilka). "What may be credited" is, in Greek, "fruit" which in this context means "profit" or "interest." "Account" is a banking term. "I have received full payment" is "a technical expression used for drawing up a receipt for payment in full discharge of a bill" (Martin). In verses 15-16 he had already begun to use such terms. There he talks about a "partnership" between him and the Philippians in which the expenditures and receipts ("giving and receiving"—these terms refer to the debit and credit sides of an accounting ledger) are accounted for.

v. 17 **Not that I am looking** . . . Paul flips back to the other side of the question: his independence.

v. 18 **even more/amply supplied** . . . Paul is pleading with them not to send further gifts.

a fragrant offering, an acceptable sacrifice . . . Paul now shifts his metaphor from the world of banking to the world of religion, specifically, to the idea of a sacrificial system. The gift to Paul was also a gift to God, similar to the sweet odor of animal sacrifice offered up to God. (See Gen. 8:20-21; Exo. 29:18.)

v. 19 . . . Ultimately, it is God who meets material needs. (Paul is still discussing the same needs here as he has been all along.) But as he has shown in verses 10-19, coping with needs involves the whole Christian family: God, self, and others. So, Paul has learned through experience to be content in whatever circumstance he finds himself (Paul's own action—vv. 11-12). Yet, it is God who gives him the strength to live like this (God's action—v. 13). At the same time, it is the Philippians who supplied his needs (the actions of others—vv. 14-16). And their needs are, in turn, supplied by God (God's action—perhaps directly, perhaps through the character he is building in them, perhaps through others—v. 19). In other words, the Christian lives within a web of inter-connected relationships.

SESSION 6
Bad Investment

Sometimes it seems like everybody is after our money. We are bombarded with requests to buy numerous products or to put our money in "sure-fire" investments. We feel like we must decide whether we want to be a "breed apart" or whether we want to "make money the old-fashioned way." Every once in a while an investment comes along which is too "good" to resist. And many of us learn first-hand what a bad investment is.

A bad investment can sting, but it also can teach us much. In addition to teaching us that we are not as smart as we thought, it can show us that money is not quite as important as we had perceived it to be. In fact, money can give us a false sense of security and power.

In the following Gospel Study, Jesus uses a parable to show how a position of "privilege" can lead to a distorted perspective on spiritual reality. If Jesus was teaching this parable today, he might say that "it's hard to be humble when you have it all." In the Epistle Study, James addresses businessmen, not to condemn them but to remind them that they must take God into account in their buying and selling.

OPTION 1

Gospel Study/Tax Audit

OPEN

STEP ONE: Complete the following exercise and share your responses with your group.

LEADER: IF YOU HAVE RE THAN SEVEN T THE MEETING, SUBDIVIDE TO GROUPS OF FOUR FOR GREATER PARTICIPATION (SEE BOX ON PAGE 6).

From the following list, indicate those areas which represent a good (G) investment of your time, energy, and/or money and those areas which represent a poor (P) investment of your time, energy, and/or money.

_____ staying in good health
_____ working to get ahead
_____ shopping
_____ giving to and volunteering for charitable activities
_____ getting more education
_____ eating and drinking with friends at a restaurant
_____ spending time with your family
_____ attending and supporting a church
_____ watching TV
_____ taking a two week vacation
_____ investing in the stock market
_____ looking for love
_____ working for financial independence

_____ starting your own business
_____ spending time with friends
_____ giving your child a good education
_____ trying to change the world
_____ trying to change other people
_____ trying to change yourself
_____ remodeling your "fixer-upper" house

STUDY | **STEP TWO: Read Luke 18:9-14** and discuss your responses to the following questions with your group.

> *⁹To some who were confident of their own righteousness and looked down on everyone else, Jesus told this parable: ¹⁰"Two men went up to the temple to pray, one was a Pharisee and the other a tax collector. ¹¹The Pharisee stood up and prayed about himself: 'God, I thank you that I am not like other men—robbers, evildoers, adulterers—or even like this tax collector. ¹²I fast twice a week and give a tenth of all I get.'*
>
> *¹³"But the tax collector stood at a distance. He would not even look up to heaven, but beat his breast and said, 'God, have mercy on me, a sinner.'*
>
> *¹⁴"I tell you that this man, rather than the other, went home justified before God. For everyone who exalts himself will be humbled, and he who humbles himself will be exalted."*
>
> *Luke 18:9-14 NIV*

1. If Jesus told this parable today, what group of people would be like the "Pharisees"? Who would be the "tax collector"? What would their respective prayers sound like?

2. What do you see as the major difference(s) between the Pharisee and the tax collector?
   a. They were from different classes of society
   b. The Pharisee was more religious
   c. The tax collector was genuinely repentant; the Pharisee was not
   d. The tax collector was more "real"

3. What is your impression of the Pharisee?
   a. He was truly seeking God
   b. He was arrogant and self-righteous
   c. He was sacrificially giving of his time and money
   d. He was "playing religion"
   e. He thought his good works would get him into heaven
   f. He would be welcome in our small group

4. What is your impression of the tax collector?
   a. He was an undesirable person
   b. He had hit "rock bottom"
   c. He had no pretense about him
   d. He would make a good friend
   e. He was truly repentant for his sins
   f. He would be welcome in our small group

5. What is/are the difference(s) in the way each of these men invested their lives?
   a. The Pharisee made his life a pursuit of God
   b. The tax collector made his life a pursuit of money
   c. The Pharisee was working his way to heaven
   d. The tax collector wanted to find God
   e. The Pharisee was living only for himself
   f. The tax collector was doing the best he could

6. Why did Jesus respond more favorably to the actions of the tax collector than to the actions of the Pharisee?
   a. Because the Pharisee wasn't giving enough money to God
   b. Because the tax collector was genuinely repentant for his sins
   c. Because the Pharisee was self-righteous and not humble
   d. Because the tax collector knew "his place"

7. What is Jesus trying to teach us through this parable?
   a. That genuine prayer is powerful
   b. That God loves true repentance
   c. That good works do not achieve salvation
   d. That true repentance leads to salvation
   e. That God hates self-righteous religion
   f. That working our way to heaven is futile
   g. That God is for the "underdog"
   h. That true humility is pleasing to God

APPLY

STEP THREE: We all have 168 hours to invest each week. From the list below and on the next page, determine how much time each week you invest in the following activities. (Since all possible activities are not covered, your total probably will not be exactly 168 hours.) Share your results with your group.

Activity	Time
Working (including housework)	_____
Eating	_____
Sleeping	_____
Attending school	_____

Activity	Time
Commuting to/from work	_____
Spending time with spouse	_____
Spending time with children	_____
Spending time with friends	_____
Attending church/church activities	_____
Exercising	_____
Playing	_____
Shopping	_____
Relaxing	_____
Watching TV	_____
Miscellaneous activities	_____
Total Hours	_____

As you look at your list, what changes, if any, would you make in the way you invest your time?

OPTION 2

Epistle Study/Business Plan

OPEN

STEP ONE: Start with the OPEN question on pages 43-44.

STUDY

STEP TWO: Read James 4:13-17 and discuss your responses to the following questions with your group. If you do not understand a word or phrase, check the Reference Notes on the next page.

> *¹³Now listen, you who say, "Today or tomorrow we will go to this or that city, spend a year there, carry on business and make money." ¹⁴Why, you do not even know what will happen tomorrow. What is your life? You are a mist that appears for a little while and then vanishes. ¹⁵Instead, you ought to say, "If it is the Lord's will, we will live and do this or that." ¹⁶As it is, you boast and brag. All such boasting is evil. ¹⁷Anyone, then, who knows the good he ought to do and doesn't do it, sins.* **James 4:13-17 NIV**

1. Are you more of a long-range planner, or do you honestly take one day at a time? Illustrate.

2. Who is James addressing in these verses?

3. Why is James "down" on planning ahead and/or making money?

4. In what ways are these verses contrary to our contemporary lifestyles?

5. In reality, how much can we dictate and determine the course of our lives?

6. What part does God play in determining the course and content of our lives?

7. Why is boasting and bragging not desirable? What then should be our attitude?

REFLECT

STEP THREE: As time allows, discuss with your group your agreement or disagreement with the following statements.

- Life is a little gleam of time between two eternities.

  — Thomas Carlyle

- Your life is like a coin. You can spend it anyway you wish, but you can spend it only once.

  — Lillian Dickson

- Life is our capital and we spend it every day. The question is, what are we getting in return?

  — Curtis Jones

APPLY

STEP FOUR: Answer the following question and share your responses with your group.

Which one of the following statements best describes how you "go at life"? Illustrate from a recent experience.

_____ Eat, drink, and be merry for tomorrow we die

_____ *"Que sera, sera"*—whatever will be, will be

_____ Who said you can't have it all?

_____ If life is a bowl of cherries, why am I always in the pits?

_____ Relax, God is in control

_____ You get out of life what you put into it

_____ By the yard, life is hard: by the inch, it's a cinch (Robert Schuller)

_____ Sit loosely in the saddle of life (Robert Louis Stevenson)

_____ Life is hard and then you die

_____ Life is 10% what happens to us and 90% how we respond to it

REFERENCE NOTES

Summary . . . James begins discussion of his third and final theme: testing. He will deal with this theme as it touches the issue of wealth. He has just spoken about a particular form of disharmony within the Christian community, that which is generated by slander and judgment (4:11–12). Now he turns to a different problem: the difficulty that comes from being wealthy and the kind of problems this brings, both on a personal level and for the whole community. In this first part of his discussion (4:13–17) he looks at the situation of a group of Christian businessmen, in particular, at their "sins of omission."

v. 13 . . . Boasting about what will happen tomorrow is another example of human arrogance. It is in the same category as judging one another (vv. 11-12). Judgment is arrogant because God is the only legitimate judge. Boasting about the future is arrogant because God is the only one who knows what will happen in the future. Such arrogance is the opposite of the humility which is supposed to characterize Christians (v. 10). It is also another sign of "friendship with the world" (v. 4).

v. 13 **Now listen** . . . This is literally "Come now." It stands in sharp contrast to the way James has been addressing his readers. In the previous section he called them "my brothers" (3:1, 11). James reverts to this more impersonal language in addressing these merchants.

"Today or tomorrow we will go . . ." James lets us listen in on the plans of a group of businessmen. Possibly they are looking at a map together. In any case, they are planning for the future and are concerned with where they will go, how long they will stay, what they will do, and how much profit they will make. It appears to be an innocent conversation. "In trade a person has to plan ahead: Travel plans, market projections, time frames, profit forecasts are the stuff of business in all ages. Every honest merchant would plan in exactly the same way—pagan, Jew, or Christian—and that is exactly the problem James has with these plans. There is absolutely nothing about their desires for the future, their use of money, or their way of doing business that is any different from the rest of the world. Their worship may be exemplary, their personal morality, impeccable; but when it comes to business they think entirely on a worldly plane" (Davids, GNC).

we will go . . . Travel by traders in the first century usually took the form of caravan or ship. There were no hard and fast time-tables. Instead, one had to wait until the right transportation came along going in your direction. However, there were certain seasons when ships sailed and caravans were more likely to travel.

carry on business . . . The word James uses here is derived from the Greek word *emporos*, from which the English word *emporium* comes. It denotes wholesale merchants who traveled from city to city, buying and selling. A different word was used to describe local peddlers who had small businesses in the bazaars. The growth of cities and the increase of trade between them during the Graeco-Roman era created great opportunities for making money. In the Bible a certain distrust of traders is sometimes expressed (see Prov. 20:23; Amos 8:4-6; Rev. 18:11-20).

v. 14 **tomorrow . . .** All such planning presupposes that tomorrow will unfold like any other day, when in fact, the future is anything but secure. (See Prov. 27:1.)

What is your life? . . . Is it not death that is the great unknown? Who can know when death will come and interrupt plans? "Their projections are made; their plans are laid. But it all hinges on a will higher than theirs, a God unconsulted in their planning. That very night disease might strike; suddenly their plans evaporate, their only trip being one on a bier to a cold grave. They are like the rich fool of Jesus' parable, who had made a large honest profit through the chance occurrences of farming. Feeling secure, he makes rational plans for a comfortable retirement. God said to him, 'You fool! This very night you will have to give up your life' (Luke 12:16-21). By thinking on the worldly plane, James' Christian business people have gained a false sense of security. They need to look death in the face and realize their lack of control over life" (Davids, GNC).

mist . . . Hosea 13:3 says: "Therefore they will be like the morning mist, like the early dew that disappears, like chaff swirling from a threshing floor, like smoke escaping through a window."

v. 15 **"If it is the Lord's will . . ."** The uncertainty of the future ought not to be a terror to the Christian. Instead, it ought to force on him/her an awareness of how dependent a person is upon God, and thus move that person to a planning that involves God. This phrase (often abbreviated D.V. after its Latin form) is not used in the Old Testament, though it was found frequently in Greek and Roman literature and is used by Paul (see Acts 18:21; 1 Cor. 4:19; 16:7).

we will live and do this or that . . . James is not ruling out planning. He says plan, but keep God in mind.

v. 16 **. . .** In contrast to such prayerful planning, these Christian merchants are very proud of what they do on their own. James is not condemning international trade as such, nor the wealth it produced. (His comments on riches come in 5:1-3.) What he is concerned about is that all this is done without reference to God, in a spirit of boastful arrogance.

boast . . . The problem with this boasting is that they are claiming to have the future under control when, in fact, it is God who holds time in his hands. These are empty claims.

brag . . . This word originally described an itinerant quack who touted "cures" that did not work. It came to mean claiming to be able to do something that you could not do.

v. 17 . . . Some feel that this proverb-like statement may, in fact, be a saying of Jesus that did not get recorded in the Gospel accounts. In any case, by it James points out the nature of so-called "sins of omission." In other words, it is sin when we fail to do what we ought to do. The more familiar definition is of "sins of commission" or wrong-doing (see 1 John 3:4). In other words, sinning can be both active and passive. Christians can sin by doing what they ought not to do (law breaking); or by not doing what they know they should do (failure).

who knows the good . . . James applies this principle to these merchants. It is not that they are cheating and stealing in the course of their business (that would be active wrong doing). The problem is what they fail to do. Generally James defines "the good" as acts of charity toward those in need. And certainly in the context of this letter it would appear that these men are failing in their duty to the poor. "James, then, may be suggesting that they plan like the world because they are motivated by the world, for God has his own way to invest money; give it to the poor (Matt. 6:19-21). If they took God into account they might not be trying to increase their own standard of living; God might lead them to relieve the suffering around them, that is, to do good" (Davids, GNC).

SESSION 7
Best Investment

Most of us want to live the best life possible. The problem is that there are no detailed road maps which instruct us concerning every step along life's journey. Instead, we are given insights from religion and philosophy which give us general directions. All of these insights attempt to answer the questions: "Who am I?" and "What am I doing here?"

When Jesus addressed these questions, he made it clear that we can know who we are and what we are doing on earth. He stated that we are created by God for the purpose of loving and serving him. Jesus clearly states in the following Gospel passage that we must decide whether we will serve God or the god of this world—money. Here, Jesus cannot be accused of subtlety. His teachings are disquieting—but they must be confronted. Jesus is calling us to invest our lives in service to him. In the Epistle Study, the Apostle Paul echoes a similar theme. As we generously invest our lives—our money, our time, our energy—in service to Christ, life becomes meaningful.

OPTION 1

Gospel Study/Service Charge

OPEN

STEP ONE: Answer the following questions and share your responses with your group.

1. Which of the following words describes your idea of a "shrewd investor"?

___ smart	___ far-sighted	___ candid
___ honest	___ careless	___ foxy
___ crafty	___ discerning	___ unsophisticated
___ fair	___ sincere	___ perceptive
___ sly	___ calculating	___ conservative
___ self-serving	___ cautious	___ shifty
___ naive		

LEADER:
IF YOU HAVE
RE THAN SEVEN
T THE MEETING,
SUBDIVIDE
TO GROUPS OF
FOUR FOR
GREATER
PARTICIPATION
(SEE BOX ON
PAGE 6).

2. Which one of the following statements best describes the way you manage your life?

___ I use others to get what I want

___ I use my resources wisely

___ I try to live a balanced life

___ I cannot manage my life; it manages me

___ I cram as much as I can into my life

___ I try to live a "laid-back" life

___ I try to invest my life in helping others

STUDY

STEP TWO: Read Luke 16:1-15 and discuss your responses to the following questions with your group.

> ¹*Jesus told his disciples: "There was a rich man whose manager was accused of wasting his possessions. ²So he called him in and asked him, 'What is this I hear about you? Give an account of your management, because you cannot be manager any longer.'*
>
> ³*"The manager said to himself, 'What shall I do now? My master is taking away my job. I'm not strong enough to dig, and I'm ashamed to beg—⁴I know what I'll do so that, when I lose my job here, people will welcome me into their houses.'*
>
> ⁵*"So he called in each one of his master's debtors. He asked the first, 'How much do you owe my master?'*
>
> ⁶*" 'Eight hundred gallons of olive oil,' he replied.*
>
> *"The manager told him, 'Take your bill, sit down quickly, and make it four hundred.'*
>
> ⁷*"Then he asked the second, 'And how much do you owe?'*
>
> *" 'A thousand bushels of wheat,' he replied.*
>
> *"He told him, 'Take your bill and make it eight hundred.'*
>
> ⁸*"The master commended the dishonest manager because he had acted shrewdly. For the people of this world are more shrewd in dealing with their own kind than are the people of the light. ⁹I tell you, use worldly wealth to gain friends for yourselves, so that when it is gone, you will be welcomed into eternal dwellings.*
>
> ¹⁰*"Whoever can be trusted with very little can also be trusted with much, and whoever is dishonest with very little will also be dishonest with much. ¹¹So if you have not been trustworthy in handling worldly wealth, who will trust you with true riches? ¹²And if you have not been trustworthy with someone else's property, who will give you property of your own?*
>
> ¹³*"No servant can serve two masters. Either he will hate the one and love the other, or he will be devoted to the one and despise the other. You cannot serve both God and Money."*
>
> ¹⁴*The Pharisees, who loved money, heard all this and were sneering at Jesus. ¹⁵He said to them, "You are the ones who justify yourselves in the eyes of men, but God knows your hearts. What is highly valued among men is detestable in God's sight."*
>
> *Luke 16:1-15 NIV*

1. What shrewd businessman or woman do you know who fits the description of the one in this story? What impresses or depresses you about either the person you know or this person whom the master commends?

2. What was the problem between the rich man and his manager?
   a. The manager was extorting money
   b. The rich man did not hold the manager accountable
   c. The rich man believed unsubstantiated rumors
   d. The manager was mismanaging his boss' possessions

3. What was the manager's response to the possibility of being fired?
   a. He moved quickly to cover his tracks
   b. He acted to get revenge on his boss
   c. He moved quickly to cut his losses and his boss' losses
   d. He tried to "wheel and deal" his way out of trouble

4. How did the manager try to remedy the situation?
   a. He made the debtors an offer they couldn't refuse
   b. He settled debtor accounts for less than full value
   c. He used "strong arm" tactics to collect the debts
   d. He took whatever the debtors would pay

5. What motivated the manager to take this action?
   a. He wanted to "short-change" his boss
   b. He wanted to create obligations he could later "call in"
   c. He wanted to avoid "hard labor"
   d. He wanted to avoid welfare

6. Why did the master commend the manager?
   a. Because some payment was better than none
   b. Because the manager had acted quickly and decisively
   c. Because the master didn't want to try to collect the debts
   d. Because he admired shrewdness

7. What was Jesus teaching through this parable?
   a. We should prepare for the future
   b. We should be shrewd for God's kingdom
   c. We should show generosity to our debtors
   d. We should use money to buy friends
   e. Power and money should be used shrewdly
   f. Dishonesty is the best policy
   g. Money can be a "substitute god"
   h. We cannot worship both God and money
   i. God detests the pursuit of wealth
   j. We are to invest our lives in serving God and not pursuing wealth

8. What is/are the difference(s) in God's value system and the human value system?
   a. God values spiritual riches
   b. We usually value money and power
   c. God values unselfish living
   d. We often take care of ourselves first

APPLY

STEP THREE: Answer the following questions and share your responses with your group.

1. Where in your life are you currently experiencing the most conflict regarding money?

2. Are you currently experiencing a conflict between earning and using money and your relationship with God? If so, how do you view this conflict?

3. What practical changes can you make in your life to make you less of a "slave" to money?

OPTION 2

Epistle Study/Living and Giving

OPEN

STEP ONE: Start with the OPEN questions on page 51.

STUDY

STEP TWO: Read 2 Corinthians 9:6-15 and discuss your responses to the following questions with your group. If you do not understand a word or phrase, check the Reference Notes on page 56.

⁶Remember this: Whoever sows sparingly will reap sparingly, and whoever sows generously will also reap generously. ⁷Each man should give what he has decided in his heart to give, not reluctantly or under compulsion, for God loves a cheerful giver. ⁸And God is able to make all grace abound to you, so that in all things at all times, having all that you need, you will abound in every good work. ⁹As it is written:

"He has scattered abroad his gifts to the poor;
his righteousness endures forever."

¹⁰Now he who supplies seed to the sower and bread for food will also supply and increase your store of seed and will enlarge the harvest of your righteousness. ¹¹You will be made rich in every way so that you can be generous on every occasion, and through us your generosity will result in thanksgiving to God.

¹²This service that you perform is not only supplying the needs of God's people but is also overflowing in many expressions of thanks to

God. ¹³Because of the service by which you have proved yourselves, men will praise God for the obedience that accompanies your confession of the gospel of Christ, and for your generosity in sharing with them and with everyone else. ¹⁴And in their prayers for you their hearts will go out to you, because of the surpassing grace God has given you. ¹⁵Thanks be to God for his indescribable gift!

2 Corinthians 9:6–15 NIV

1. What is one lesson about money you can recall learning from your parents?

2. As for Paul's lesson: If you invest sparingly, what is the result? If we invest generously, what is the result? Is Paul saying that, if we give $100, we will get back $1000? Why or why not?

3. What should be our motivation in generously sharing what we have?

4. What is God's response to a generous giver?

5. Why shouldn't we be concerned about our basic needs?

6. What is the relationship between generosity and righteousness?

7. How do our acts of generosity affect the way other people view God?

8. In what ways is the generous and wise investment of our lives a gift from God?

REFLECT

STEP THREE: As time allows, discuss with your group your agreement or disagreement with the following statements.

• He that is of the opinion money will do everything may well be suspected of doing everything for money.

— *Benjamin Franklin*

• To meet Jesus is to look yourself in the pocketbook, which is the most unmistakable way of looking yourself in the heart.

— *J. Robert Ross*

APPLY

STEP FOUR: Answer the following questions and share your responses with your group.

1. Which one of the following words best describes you as a "giver"?

____ openhanded	____ lavish	____ sporadic
____ liberal	____ generous	____ extravagant
____ tightfisted	____ frugal	____ unselfish
____ bighearted	____ calculated	____ reluctant
____ cheerful	____ thankful	____ charitable
____ closefisted		

2. If you were paid $10.00/hour for every loving thing you did for someone else last week, and if you had to pay out the same wages to anyone who likewise showed generosity to you, would you come out a debtor or a creditor by week's end?

3. In what ways do you think God is asking you to become more generous with your money, time, and energy?

Summary . . . Paul concludes his section on the collection with his general exhortation to give generously.

REFERENCE NOTES

v. 6 . . . It sounds almost as if Paul is quoting a proverb, though the source of his words (if any) is not clear. In any case, what he says is quite obvious: if a farmer sows only a few seeds he can't expect a bountiful crop. By this illustration from nature he encourages generous giving. In verses 7–15 he will spell out just what it is that the Christian does harvest by giving.

v. 7 . . . Having encouraged generosity, Paul next urges cheerfulness in that giving. The giver ought not to feel pressured but should simply give what it is that has been laid on his/her heart to give.

God loves . . . i.e., God approves.

a cheerful giver . . . Paul quotes Proverbs 22:8.

v. 8 . . . "The sense of the verse seems to be that if men are willing to give, God will always make it possible for them to give" (Barrett).

having all that you need . . . The Greek word underlying this phrase does not mean having a great abundance of possessions. Rather, it is used to describe a person who is able to live on very little and therefore has few wants. Such a person is then able to give away a great deal to meet the needs of others. See Philippians 4:11 where Paul uses a related word to describe such a lifestyle.

v. 9 . . . Paul quotes from Psalm 112:9 to show that it is important to give to the poor and that this giving has an abiding moral quality to it.

vv. 10–11 . . . Drawing upon Isaiah 55:10 and Hosea 10:12 Paul makes two points about God. He supplies the basic needs of people and then he prospers these gifts when they are used. Paul then uses this illustration to make his point about giving, but he does it in reverse fashion. In verse 10b he points out that one's moral well-being (or "harvest of righteousness") is enhanced by God as a result of cheerful giving. In verse 11 he parallels 10a and points out that just as it is Christ who supplies the seed, so too he supplies the financial means by which one is enabled to give.

v. 11 **You will be made rich . . .** The purpose of such riches is to facilitate generosity, not to pamper personal indulgences. Notice how God meets the needs of the poor by supplying riches to others to give. God could simply fulfill each person's needs directly but instead works through others, for the reasons Paul will enumerate in verses 12–14.

thanksgiving . . . Such giving to the poor overflows into praise to God because the poor gratefully thank God (v. 13).

v. 12 **service . . .** in Greek *diakonia*, the word from which *deacon* is derived.

perform . . . In Greek *leitourgia*, from which the English word *liturgy* comes. It carries the idea of public service and was used to describe volunteer service rendered by wealthy citizens to others. It is virtually synonymous with *diakonia*. Such giving is not like the Jewish temple tax which a person was required to pay. Rather, it is a voluntary act done on behalf of a needy other. In Judaism it was used to describe religious service.

needs of God's people . . . The poor are actually helped. This is one fruit of generosity.

vv. 13–14 . . . Paul explains how giving creates thanksgiving: 1) People praise God because of the obedience they see in his people. ("Christianity really works. See how they care for the poor." This insight on the part of the needy Jewish Christians would cause them to see that the faith of the Gentile Christians is real.) 2) The needy praise God because he has answered their prayers and met their needs. 3) They pray for and offer themselves to their benefactors (not because of the giver's inherent "goodness" but because of God's grace which has caused them to give) and this, presumably, causes the givers to praise God because of the resulting warmth of fellowship. Giving is good for the health of the whole church!

v. 15 . . . In fact, Paul himself is moved to offer this very sort of thanks to God: Thanks for the gift of *grace* given them that produced Christians of this sort; and also thanks for the *gift of Jesus Christ* (8:9) whose work of reconciliation made such changed hearts possible.

Suggested Reading

Master Your Money: a Step-By-Step Plan For Financial Freedom, Ron Blue, Nashville: T. Nelson Publishers, 1986.

Money Matter, R.C. Sproul, Wheaton, IL: Tyndale House Publishers, 1985.

Money, Sex, and Power, Richard J. Foster, San Francisco: Harper and Row, 1985.

Rich Christians In An Age Of Hunger: A Biblical Study, Ronald J. Sider, Downers Grove, IL: Inter-Varsity Press, 1984.

Your Money Or Your Life: A New Look At Jesus' View Of Wealth And Power, San Francisco: Harper and Row, 1986.